XL MACHINES
GARBAGE TRUCKS

MARIE MORRISON

New York

Published in 2020 by The Rosen Publishing Group, Inc.
29 East 21st Street, New York, NY 10010

Copyright © 2020 by The Rosen Publishing Group, Inc.

All rights reserved. No part of this book may be reproduced in any form without permission in writing from the publisher, except by a reviewer.

First Edition

Editor: Elizabeth Krajnik
Book Design: Michael Flynn

Photo Credits: Cover, p. 1 SunChan/E+/Getty Images; series background (dirt) exopixel/Shutterstock.com; p. 5 Mint Images/Mint Images RF/Getty Images; p. 7 Bettmann/Getty Images; p. 9 Johnny Habell/Shutterstock.com; p. 11 Baloncici/Shutterstock.com; p. 13 Rob Crandall/Shutterstock.com; p. 15 Nitikorn Poonsiri/Shutterstock.com; p. 17 Julien McRoberts/Getty Images; p. 19 kaband/Shutterstock.com; p. 21 Paul Vasarhelyi/Shutterstock.com; p. 22 Nerthuz/Shutterstock.com.

Cataloging-in-Publication Data

Names: Morrison, Marie.
Title: Garbage trucks / Marie Morrison.
Description: New York : PowerKids Press, 2020. | Series: XL machines! | Includes glossary and index.
Identifiers: ISBN 9781725311541 (pbk.) | ISBN 9781725311565 (library bound) | ISBN 9781725311558 (6pack)
Subjects: LCSH: Refuse collection vehicles-Juvenile literature. | Refuse and refuse disposal-Juvenile literature.
Classification: LCC TD794.M677 2020 | DDC 628.4'42-dc23

Manufactured in the United States of America

CPSIA Compliance Information: Batch #CSPK19. For Further Information contact Rosen Publishing, New York, New York at 1-800-237-9932.

CONTENTS

Cleaning Up 4
Garbage History 6
The Dempster Dumpster 8
Compact It! 10
Front and Back 12
How Huge? 14
Follow the Trash 16
To the Landfill! 18
Be Safe! 20
Help Out 22
Glossary 23
Index 24
Websites 24

Cleaning Up

There's just something special about **garbage** trucks. Right on time, often once a week, they show up to take away our garbage. Sometimes they take the things we recycle, too. They're often loud, sometimes a little smelly, and always useful!

Garbage History

In the 20th century, people started using trucks that took garbage to the dump. These trucks had open backs, though. Garbage could fly out, and they really smelled! The kinds of garbage trucks we commonly see today were first used during the 1930s.

The Dempster Dumpster

In 1937, a man named George Dempster invented a new kind of garbage truck. Garbage workers filled bins called dumpsters with trash. Then they emptied the bins into the trucks using special machinery. The trucks were covered, so trash couldn't fly out as easily.

Compact It!

Not long after the Dempster Dumpster system started, there was another change to garbage trucks. They could use machines to **compact** the garbage! When the trash is compacted, there's more room in the truck. The trucks can carry more garbage on each trip.

Front and Back

Today, there are still two main kinds of garbage trucks. There are front-loader trucks, which still work with dumpsters. And there are rear-loader trucks, in which garbage workers throw garbage into the rear of the trucks. Sometimes, there are side-loaders, too.

How Huge?

Garbage trucks come in many sizes. Most empty trucks weigh about 33,000 pounds (14,968.5 kg). They'll weigh 50,000 pounds (22,679 kg) with garbage. That's a lot of trash! Some big trucks can weigh up to 80,000 pounds (36,287 kg).

Follow the Trash

After a garbage truck picks up your garbage, it carries it to different places. Sometimes, it goes to a place where workers take out waste that can be recycled. These things include plastic bottles, some paper, and **metal**. They may be turned into new things.

To the Landfill!

Garbage trucks take most trash to **landfills**. These are big lined pits in the ground that hold garbage. Once each pit is full, it's covered up. Some of the trash will break down in the landfill. Sometimes, though, this takes a very long time.

Be Safe!

It can be interesting to watch the garbage truck as it moves down your street. But these are huge machines. Be sure never to play, stand, or ride your bike behind a garbage truck. Stand back and wave if you want to say hi!

Help Out

The **average** person in the United States produces about 4.4 pounds (2 kg) of trash a day. That's a lot for garbage trucks to carry! Make sure to recycle what you can. There still will be things for garbage trucks to carry, but fewer things for landfills!

GLOSSARY

average: Being much like other things of a kind.

compact: To force closer together.

garbage: Things that have been thrown out; trash.

landfill: A place where garbage is buried.

metal: A hard, shiny matter found in the ground, such as iron or copper.

INDEX

D
Dempster, George, 8, 10
dump, 6
dumpsters, 8, 10, 12

F
front-loader trucks, 12

G
garbage, 4, 6, 8, 10, 12, 14, 16, 18

L
landfills, 18, 22

M
metal, 16

P
paper, 16
plastic bottles, 16

R
rear-loader trucks, 12

S
side-loader trucks, 12

U
United States, 22

WEBSITES

Due to the changing nature of Internet links, PowerKids Press has developed an online list of websites related to the subject of this book. This site is updated regularly. Please use this link to access the list: www.powerkidslinks.com/xlm/garbagetrucks